STRATEGIC LEADERSHIP

Leading Change in a New Age

STRATEGIC LEADERSHIP

Leading Change in a New Age

Joseph KingJr., EdD

Order this book online at **www.trafford.com**
or email orders@trafford.com

Most Trafford titles are also available at major online book retailers.

Printed in the United States of America.

ISBN: 978-1-4269-7534-9 (sc)
ISBN: 978-1-4269-7535-6 (hc)
ISBN: 978-1-4269-7536-3 (e)

Library of Congress Control Number: 2011911507

Trafford rev. 07/15/2011

 **www.trafford.com**

North America & International
toll-free: 1 888 232 4444 (USA & Canada)
phone: 250 383 6864 ♦ fax: 812 355 4082

ACKNOWLEDGEMENTS

I want to recognize the inspiration support and leadership provided to me by the late Mr. and Mrs. Joseph and Jessie King, my parents and family members that supported me in this endeavor.

ABSTRACT

Joseph King, Jr., Ed.D.

Strategic Leadership: Leading Change in a New Age

A Strategy Research Project

This research paper documents strategic leadership requirements and initiatives for transformation of the U.S. Army for the 21st Century. The key leadership areas are strategic planning, customers, information, human resources, process improvement, business results and innovation and change. Force XXI and Army After Next (AAN) initiatives lead change now to actualize the vision of the 21st Century. The thesis in this paper is: strategic leadership is imperative in leading change and transforming the Army for the 21st Century (new age). After World War II the U.S. government provided technology transfer to the private or commercial sector. In today's environment the reverse is true, the commercial sector is primarily providing technology transfer to the government and the Department of Defense. Although war fighting is the province of the military, much can be learned from the commercial sector to improve process, adopt best practices and achieve the visions of Force XXI, AAN and Joint Vision 2010. Strategic leadership is paramount in leading change.

CONTENTS

ACKNOWLEDGEMENTS v
ABSTRACT..vii
STRATEGIC LEADERSHIP: LEADING CHANGE
    IN A NEW AGE..1
INTRODUCTION...3
LEADERSHIP – STRATEGIC ART..6
DECISION MAKING 7
STRATEGIC PLANNING 9
CUSTOMER AND MARKET FOCUS 12
INFORMATION AND ANALYSIS..15
HUMAN RESOURCES..18
PROCESS MANAGEMENT 22
BUSINESS RESULTS 25
LEADING INNOVATION AND CHANGE................................29
SERVANT LEADERSHIP 35
CONCLUSION 37
ENDNOTES..39
BIBLIOGRAPHY..43

LIST OF ILLUSTRATIONS

Figure 1 Core and Supporting Themes 10
Figure 2 Strategic Preclusion 11
Figure 3 Assessment 12
Figure 4 Army Imperatives 13
Figure 5 Strategic Decision Making Challenges 19
Figure 6 Consensus Team Decision Making Process 20
Figure 7 Total Quality Management 23
Figure 8 Flow Diagram 24
Figure 9 Leader Competencies 37

STRATEGIC LEADERSHIP: LEADING CHANGE IN A NEW AGE

It is necessary to develop a strategy that utilizes all the physical conditions and elements that are directly at hand. The best strategy relies upon an unlimited set of responses....

--Morihei Ueshiba

INTRODUCTION

Strategic leadership is a concept which will direct change into the 21st Century and beyond. Key in building organizations with a focus on the future is the vision of a positive end state. This visioning process enables the leader to develop goals, objectives and plans to reach the desired goal or end state. Joint Vision 2010 also foresees the implementation of land power as a key element in fully implementing the Goldwater/Nichols Act. Again, research documents the key areas necessary for organization systemic change that optimizes strategy, missions, capabilities, resources and people. In transforming the Army into an organization that can meet the goals of Force XXI and the Army After Next (AAN), the leader must counter a "zero defects" mentality and utilize competencies and tasks which respond to the current environment which is volatile, uncertain, complex and ambiguous (VUCA). To lead change in a VUCA environment the Army must begin to realize the end state developed which, by the way, is constantly evolving and ever changing. In fact, the only constant in the environment is change. If change occurs no matter what we do, then the leader must direct the change toward the envisioned end state. Three key principles in leading change in the 21st Century are empowerment, environment, and the golden rule.[1] To achieve an end state that achieves the objectives of Army XXI, AAN and Joint Vision 2010, the principles of war must guide war fighting at the strategic, operational and tactical levels and must be incorporated in organizational transformations.[2] I will develop a concept which will address the requirements and initiatives necessary for leading change in the 21st Century. To refine the discussion, analysis and conclusions the research will address the 1998 Army performance

Improvement Criteria (APIC). The Army APIC is a separate Chief of Staff Army initiative to enhance quality in the Army as a whole. The Army After Next (AAN) is another Chief of Staff Army initiative that seeks to achieve a year 2025 end state by starting to vision and achieve the end state now. These programs and concepts are separate and distinct. Although they are both Chief of Staff Army initiatives, they had never been integrated. Two distinct initiatives are integrated as a concept framework for achieving a desired end state. The paper does not attempt to currently assess the progress of AAN, however, the paper discusses in-depth how the APIC criteria can be integrated in the strategic leadership initiatives of AAN. Perhaps the integration of the two concepts can assist in assessing some quantitative and qualitative aspects of the AAN initiative. Due to the outstanding results of the APIC in the commercial sector, I believe the Army and AAN can become more effective as an organization. The key areas of focus will be:

- Leadership
- Strategic Planning
- Customer and Market Focus
- Information and Analysis
- Human Resources
- Process Management
- Business Results
- Leading Change and Innovations

The APIC are derived from the Malcolm Balridge National Quality Award Criteria for performance excellence.

The APIC rewords the criteria for performance excellence to fit the unique nature of the Army mission: to deter aggression, to fight and win the nation's wars, and to provide a range of military options short of war. . . . "The APIC connects elements of combat power (maneuver, fire power, protection, and leadership) created by Army table of distribution and allowances (TDA) organizations in peacetime to the elements of combat power created by Army tables of organization and equipment (TO&E) units during war and military operations other than war (MOOTW). Efficiently managed child care centers, post range operations, digitized classrooms, acquisition operations, enable individual soldiers and tactical units to accomplish their missions before, during and after war".[3]

This quotation reveals that the current Army criteria is applied to all types of units in the Army such as combat, combat service, and combat service support.

LEADERSHIP – STRATEGIC ART

The 21st Century will require innovation in leadership to meet the end state as envisioned in the year 2025. A new discipline that enhances the leadership requirements for the 21st Century is the strategic art. Strategic art, broadly defined, is:

> . . . the skillful formation, coordination, and application of ends (objectives), ways (courses of action) , and means (supporting resources) to promote and defend the national interests. . . . The "strategic art entails the orchestration of all the instruments of national power to yield specific, well-defined end states. Desired end states and strategic outcomes derive from the national interests and are variously defined in terms of physical security, economic well-being, and the promotion of values".[4]

This reveals that strategic art is the cornerstone of strategic leadership. Leadership must guide any long-range initiative, particularly AAN. A practitioner of the strategic art becomes the complete strategist, this requires the performance of three distinct roles: the strategic leader, strategic practitioner, and strategic theorist.[5] This new discipline is key in transforming the Army to arrive at the desired end state in 2025 and beyond. This leadership capability is imperative in achieving organizational excellence in a rapidly changing volatile, uncertain, complex, and ambiguous (VUCA) environment.

DECISION MAKING

I have framed the current and future environment as VUCA, the response to challenges must ensure strategic leadership applies to decision making that achieves results and the desired objectives. "Strategic decisions have the following characteristics:
- Consequential, not unimportant
- Long-term, not shortsighted
- System-wide. not stove piped
- Contextual, not structural
- Rarely final"[6]

There are also several obstacles to effective strategic decision making:
- Shortsighted vision of policy makers
- Disagreement on desired end state
- Incomplete knowledge of relevant factors
- Mis-estimation of policy effects
- Incomplete understanding of system dynamics
- Incomplete understanding of cross culture effects
- Partisan resources competition
- Mismanagement of the decision making process[7]

The previous characteristics and obstacles to effective strategic leadership and decision making reveal the impact and necessity to move from direct, tactical and operational decision making to strategic decision making which impacts the system over the long term based on the end state.

Strategic decision making is the ability to think insightfully about consequential events over time, to understand what causes long-range effects in and on complex and dynamic systems, and to bring partisan, competing interests together under shared goals.[8]

Finally, strategic leadership and decision making requires broad scope and scale, it is a process of setting the direction through negotiation, conciliation, and persuasion (i.e., consensus building) with support from constituencies required for the commitment and resources.

STRATEGIC PLANNING

The strategic planning process sets the direction and the action plans necessary to arrive at the desired future-or-end-state. The process might use models, forecasts, scenarios and intelligence to arrive at the desired end state. The AAN mission statement addresses the:

> . . . "conduct of broad studies of warfare to about the year 2025 to frame issues vital to the development of the U.S. Army after about 2010 and provide those issues to senior Army leadership in a format suitable for integration into the Training and Doctrine Command combat development programs".[9]

The FY99 campaign plan addresses the ideas, insights, and concepts for a potential force. Various war game studies and research are a part of the process that exists to facilitate the orderly development of future ideas into today's reality. The planning actions are as follows:

- Keep the Army imperatives in balance over time.
- Focus Army R&D efforts.
- Narrow gap between heavy and light forces.
- Improve mobility, enhance firepower.
- Leverage the work already done in OSD's RMA studies.
- Identify organizational concepts that better integrate the active component and the reserve component.
- Revolutionize logistical concepts. Continue developing total asset visibility and velocity management.
- Institutionalize AAN concepts and process.
- Think joint, and involve other services in the AAN process.[10]

The Chief of Staff, Army (CSA) planning guidance provides the strategic development process and the overall grand strategy to achieve the AAN end state. The mission and action plan address the overall organizational strategy, including changes in services, products, and product lines. The aforementioned strategy should be integrated broadly. The CSA's planning guidance provides the framework for subordinate organizations to understand and achieve the CSA's intent. The FY99 AAN campaign plan also provides the structure, core and supporting themes to achieve the end state. The core themes and supporting themes are depicted in Figure 1.

CORE THEMES

- Army of 2025 as a hybrid force
- Knowledge and creed
- Jointness and interdependence
- Regional engagement operations
- Capabilities Technology enables: Evolutionary and Revolutionary

SUPPORTING THEMES

- Homeland defense, AC/RC integration, urban/complex terrain
- Battle force operations
- Strike force and campaign force operations

Figure 1 Core and Supporting Themes

The aforementioned structure, core and subordinate themes provide the action plans, how they are deployed and how performance will be tracked. More importantly, the estimate how the organization will project itself in the future and achieve its mission.[11] The annual report to the CSA tracks performance. Finally, the emerging Army concepts center on a long-term view; as depicted in Figure 2.

STRATEGIC PRECLUSION
- Advanced full dimensional operations
- Immediate, simultaneous application of joint interdiction and maneuver
- Enemy concedes or is set up for failure in the face of follow on forces
- An end to end concept, operationalized in the near to mid term and fully realized with AAN and other service future capabilities

---

Figure 2 Strategic Preclusion

CUSTOMER AND MARKET FOCUS

This improvement criterion examines how requirements, expectations, and preferences of customers and markets are determined. At the tactical and operational level commanders have a plethora of feedback mechanisms that determine requirements, expectations and preferences of customers (i.e., internal and external, employees, subordinate organizations and headquarters as well as technical chains). These internal and external customers are assessed in a variety of ways. Some of the following are noteworthy as depicted in Figure 3.

ASSESSMENT
• Congressional Inquiries
• Inspector General Surveys
• Review and Analysis
• Internal Review
• Climate Assessment
• Program Analysis and Evaluation (PA&E)
• Individual Performance Ratings
• Officers and Enlisted Evaluation Report

Figure 3 Assessment

At the strategic level the AAN annual report to the CSA and Commander, Training and Doctrine Command (TRADOC) provide the customer and market focus and it relates to end state objectives to include material. The Army Experimentation Campaign Plan (AECP) and AAN provide a balanced approach to near term modernization and long term study and planning. The AECP drives the following Army imperatives as depicted in Figure 4.

ARMY IMPERATIVES
- Trained and Ready
- Quality People
- Training
- Force Mix
- Doctrine
- Modern Equipment
- Leader Development

Figure 4 Army Imperatives

In addition, APIC was developed and implemented to provide a strategic framework for leading change. It also raises performance expectations and standards and establishes cutting edge business practices as common performance criteria for operational and institutional Army organizations.[12] Customer and market knowledge is documented through the aforementioned feedback mechanisms. Leader development, an Army imperative, provides relationship enhancement. However there are still challenges that address the total Army team, (i.e., active component, the reserve component, DA civilians and contractors). Another key challenge in this area is the integration of jointness (other services and DOD agencies).

The dilemma of jointness and Army independence is the classic challenge of independence versus interdependence. Undoubtedly, this will be one of the greatest challenges to AAN.

Of all of the Baldridge Award criteria, none is more important than customer focus and satisfaction. This category accounts for 300 of the 1000 point value of the award.[13]

Again, leadership is imperative in driving customer satisfaction and achieving the end state which is based on results. If internal and external customers are satisfied, particularly in a volunteer Army, then the desired results will be achieved. The following are key excellence indicators for customer satisfaction:
- Service standards derived from customer requirements

- Understanding customer requirements
- Thoroughness/objectivity
- Customer types
- Product/service features
- Front line empowerment
- Strategic infrastructure support for frontline employees
- Attention to hiring, training, attitude, morale for front line employees
- High levels of satisfaction – customer awards
- Proactive customer service systems
- Proactive management of relationships with the customer
- Use of all listening posts
- Surveys
- Product/service follow-ups
- Complaints (i.e., IG,EO, EEO, customer)
- Turnover of customers
- Employees
- Quality requirements of market segments
- Surveys go beyond current customers
- Commitment to customers (trust/confidence/making good on word)[14]

The aforementioned indicators have to be directed from the top of the organization and inculcated throughout the chain of command.

The following quote provides a detailed three point discussion of the current Chief of Staff's leadership philosophy. This is important because it sets the direction for and provides guidance for the AAN and APIC initiatives. These initiatives are again disjointed but can be integrated to improve organization effectiveness.

My leadership philosophy is very simple. It can be summed up in three basic pointes. First, if we empower people to do what is legally and morally right, there is no limit to the good we can accomplish. . . . The second point of my leadership philosophy is to create an environment where people can be all they can be. . . . The third point in my leadership philosophy is to treat others as you would have them treat you. A leader must have compassion – a basic respect for the dignity of each individual; treating all with dignity and respect.[15]

INFORMATION AND ANALYSIS

This performance improvement criteria examines the selection, management and effectiveness of the use of information and data to support organizational processes, plans and performance management. The previously mentioned feedback mechanisms go beyond a customer focus and also address the performance management system.

An organization selects metrics that measure performance and that directly support their strategy and goals. . . . Firstly, how does the organization measure performance, Secondly, why were those measures (metrics) selected? Finally, how do the performance measures relate to the organization's priorities and drive performance?[16]

Although not all elements of AAN are subject to quantification, some are (i.e., performance management). However, this quote only highlights metrics can be used to analyze the impact of cost and the benefits and how it relates to organization performance.

Continuous improvement in an organization's processes over time, chart the course to goal attainment and achievement of the desired end state. However, metrics alone are not enough; the metrics have to be related to business results. The link between metrics and business results will be discussed in detail later in this paper. The use of information and analysis is important in focusing on targets and process actions. Best in class standards, best practices, and benchmarks drive the organization's strategy and fulfill the CSA and the Secretary of the Army's intent.

A current challenge, which has far-reaching implications for Army 2010 and AAN, is the ability to improve the bottom line. The Department of Defense Review Initiative Directive No. 20 (DRID 20) requires that Army out source to the commercial sector key functions that are not "essentially governmental." This term, "essentially governmental," is important in determining what services and functions will be out sourced or contracted out. Key in this determination is information and analysis that impacts the cost and the way business is conducted. The Army determinations will obviously be subject to review. However, it appears that it would be in the Army "best interests" to make the right determination the first time, rather than be directed by the Department of Defense (DOD) to out source functions that might impact economies of scale, efficiencies and the strategic objective. On the other hand it is important to vigorously defend those decisions not to out source. The impact of this improvement criteria is perhaps one of the Army's greatest challenges in achieving the end state objectives of 2010 and AAN. The second, third, and fourth order effects is to obtain information about information. Specially, information related to the following processes/activities:

- Army information operations
- Interservice and joint information operations
- Defense Information Infrastructure
- National Information Infrastructure
- Global Information Infrastructure[17]

Again, the metrics used to assess continuous improvement on process activity that relates to information operations and information warfare are key in driving the necessary process in achieving the desired objective of information superiority. Significant research has documented that information assurance is the Achilles' Heel of Joint Vision 2010.

The DOD infrastructure consists of over 2.1 million computers, 10,000 local area networks, and 1000 long distance networks. JV 2010 drives efforts to further interconnect these systems and migrate toward a network centric environment. Over 95% of DOD's systems utilize public communications networks available to the general public. These networks are classified as the global, national, and defense information (GH, N11, D11). Although these names imply independence, they all use interconnected transport mediums linked to public switches that route data between geographically separated systems. This includes DOD's classified systems that operate on the Secret Internet Protocol

Routing Network or SIPRNET. The multitude of automated systems allows DOD to command, control, protect, pay, supply, and inform the force. As dependence on increasingly interconnected information grows, so does DOD's vulnerability.[18]

The quote reveals the vulnerability of the DOD's information operations network. It reveals the need for quality enhancement in this area which appears to be lacking. Without the continuous improvement of processes in the vital area, it will continue to be a key vulnerability. Although the previous quote primarily focuses on the joint information assurance issues, the Army must have the same concerns to continuously improve the process and enhance productivity and goal attainment that relates to other APIC's.

HUMAN RESOURCES

This improvement criteria examines how the organization enables employees and soldiers to develop, use their potential, aligned with the organization's objectives. A key emphasis in examining this criteria is to further work design. It is also true that the compensation is also important, however, it is regulated by Congress, albeit work design and recognition are the purview of the organizations' senior leaders.

Total quality does not seem to have been instituted throughout the Army system. Although there are installations of excellence, total quality seems to have been degraded with the draw down and the current office may not be sufficiently staffed to address systemic transformation. Although, process action teams are in place, I am not aware of any organization wide determination on the "State of Total Quality." The Army is a highly complex matrix organization with combat, combat support and combat service support command organizations units, and activities. In most combat service support organizations the work designs could enhance employee involvement and develop the appropriate structures, albeit different from the war fighter's, that truly make base operations and installations power projection platforms.

Many technologies utilized in the private sector today can be transferred to the Army. In the areas of human technology, intellectual property and work design the Army may benefit from a variety of work designs just as there is a variety of pay systems structures, personnel systems to include recognition systems.

Installation key process teams, process action teams, or mechanized infantry company – teams conducting attacks at the National Training Center, promote the concepts of team work, empowerment, flexibility, and employee/soldier involvement to solve installation or tactical problems.[19]

The following challenges await the Army's strategic decision making team capability as depicted in Figure 5.

STRATEGIC DECISION MAKING CHALLENGES
- Diverse team membership
- Lack of policy guidance
- Low team authority
- Internal politics
- Organizational inertia
- Gaps and ambiguities

Figure 5 Strategic Decision Making Challenges

Given these challenges, it should be no surprise that team meetings can be a journey into foreign territory for each team member. By adopting a 'consensus style' of leadership, some of these problems can be eliminated.[20]

Consensus in strategic decision making is an area ripe for adoption by the Army. However, it requires a leap ahead in structure and be adopted Army wide.

In addition, the Army culture may prevent this type of strategic decision making capability. The commercial sector has had success and it appears the National Defense University supports a "consensus style" of leadership.

Decision making at the strategic level hinges on the ability of decision making teams to forge consensus for action. No team can succeed unless it is strong enough to sustain decisions through bureaucratic politics, interest group resistance, media criticism, and implementation. Consensus acts as the 'power plant' within the national security decision making system, or the private sector to sustain policy decisions through implementation either in the government bureaucracy, or in the market place.[21]

Finally, it is quite easy to determine challenges without courses of action. To fully redesign the work process at the operational and tactical levels is double. However, it is far more challenging to achieve the same objective at the strategic level. It is challenging due to the autonomy of senior leaders, the complexity involved in the interagency process, and more importantly, structure and process must accommodate this style of decision making. This is also due to the volatile, uncertain, complex, and ambiguous environment. However, the following process can attain strategic consensus decision making as depicted in Figure 6.

CONSENSUS TEAM DECISION MAKING PROCESS

High Conceptional Level Pillar	Factors
	Envision goals
	Design process plan
	Achieve situation assessment
	Expand frames of reference
	Focus time horizons
	Clarify value tradeoffs
	Detect gaps and ambiguity
Prudent Consensus Approach Pillar	**Factors**
	Strengthen team identity
	Control internal politics
	Foster competitive debate
	Forge consensus for action
Vigilant Decision Management Pillar	**Factors**
	Keep pace with the environment
	Manage time
	Adjust and self-correct

Source: National Defense University, Strategic leadership, and decision making. Prepare senior executives for the 21st Century. National Defense University Press, 1997, Washington, D.C.

Figure 6 Consensus Team Decision Making Process

Finally, the process for making strategic decisions is just as important as the decision itself. Critical and creative thinking skills are paramount in each individual that participates in consensus decision making at the strategic level. These directly relate to the human resource focus of performance improvement criteria, in that it directly addresses work design inputs into the continuous improvement process. Employee/soldier training and development must be conducted continuously to prepare employees/soldiers for the 21st Century. Work design, process, and worker self-management and soldier improvement must become a part of the total improvement process to prepare the organization for its 21st Century challenges. Training and development and doctrine must be transformed and aligned with 21st Century goals and objectives that lead to 2010 and AAN. Employee and soldier satisfaction and well being can engender commitment, loyalty and morale.

Approaches for supporting and enhancing employee/soldier well being, satisfaction and motivation, which might include counseling, career development and employability services, recreational or cultural activities, non-work related education, day care, job sharing, special leave for family responsibilities and/or community service, safety off the job, flexible work hours, out placement, and retiree benefits including extended health care.[22]

PROCESS MANAGEMENT

This performance improvement criterion examines process management, customer focused design, product and service delivery, service and partnering process involving all work units. Process can have many meanings. Generally it refers how products and services are developed and performed. Process depicts the how and why something works. The management of process quality is paramount. Process includes mission planning, PPBES and lessons learned. Process also spells out what must be done and how it's done. In knowledge work such as planning, research and analysis process does not imply sequential steps. Here process can imply general understanding regarding professional performance objectives. Statistical process control (SPC) can be applied to industries to provide stability and limit variation. To achieve strategic objectives, the CSA/Secretary must adopt and adapt a total quality management system that achieves the following as depicted in Figure 7.

TOTAL QUALITY MANAGEMENT

- Implement strategic quality management, including market segment differentiation based on customer expectations.
- Communicate a culture of quality throughout the organization.
- Organize the potential for world class competition.
- Integrate
- The special interest functions of the company
- The stream of processes and provide a basis for process design and control.
- Suppliers and customers.
- Everyone in the process while promoting a team culture with interfunctional teams.

Source: National Defense University, Strategic leadership, and decision making. Prepare senior executives for the 21st Century. National Defense University Press, 1997, Washington, D.C.

Figure 7 Total Quality Management

Obviously, this appears to be a lot to drive toward strategic ends. However, the previous requirements need not be a "program," but the method (course of action) of doing business in the organization. Proponents of quality function deployment (QFD) propose that this method can achieve the desired outcomes. QFD unfolds in the following steps:

Step 1 Product planning; Step 2 Prioritize; Step 3 Competitive evaluation; Step 4 The design process; Step 5 Design; Step 6 Design; Step 7 Process planning; and Step 8 Process control. When the QFD is 'deployed' the hows of one step become the 'whats' of the next one step.[23]

The sequencing of the previous steps is key in achieving desired outcomes. Often discussions of quality at the strategic level are conceptual rather than practical. The step by step process helps provide an "in process review" and can provide a qualitative assessment for continuous improvement.

The human element of statistical process control (SPC) is key in gaining commitment to the culture change effort. This is done by encouraging participation. The ownership of the processes leads to the empowerment and self-management of the soldier/employee. Social dimension of organization is enhanced. Morale improves, loyalty is enhanced and turnover is lessened. Thus the problems of managing streams of processes are both methodological and organizational. "Peter Drucker contends that SPC has its greatest impact on the factory's social organization."[24]

As SPC enhances the organizations processes to improve a product or service, it also has an impact on the human dimension and the social interactions of the workers.

Deming believed that organization transformation that impacts control of process is in the purview of management, and that only senior management can institute Process management which transforms the organization to achieve its end state. Every activity, every job is a part of a process. A flow diagram of any process will divide the work into stages. The stages as a whole form a process. The stages are now individual entities, each running at maximum profit. A flow diagram, simple or complex, is an example of a theory – an idea.

Flow Diagram
---> Stage 1 ---> Stage 2 ---> Stage 3 --->

Figure 8 Flow Diagram

Work comes into any stage, changes state, and moves on into the next stage. Any stage has a customer, the next stage. The final stage will send product or service to the ultimate customer, he that buys the product or the service. "this is what I can do for you. Here is what you might do for me." [25]

BUSINESS RESULTS

This category examines the organization's performance and improvement in a variety of areas – customer satisfaction, financial/ market place performance, human resources results, supplier and partners and operations. Various brigade units at the National Training Center provide data to the Commanding General (primary customer) in the form of After Action Reviews (AAR). The battalion commanders (primary partners) are also customers that are responsible for the processes that bring about business results. Performance improvement must be results driven, that is the goals must lead to objectives. The results (outcomes) must lead toward the desired effect. To achieve the organization's 2010 and AAN goals a new customers orientation which results in unity of effort and unity of command must drive objectives. Just as information technology is being viewed as a new way of doing business, it is being adopted also without question due to the inculcation of this technology throughout society and globally. Dr. Deeming believed that the primary reason why the commercial sector is robust (i.e., stock market, information technology advances) is due to the adoption of the new philosophy.

Adopt the new philosophy. We are in a new economic age. Western management must awaken to the challenge, must learn their responsibilities, and take on leadership for change. Put everybody in the company to work to accomplish the transformation. The transformation is everybody's job.[26]

The previous quote highlights the customer focus in that everybody in the company is a customer for everybody else. To measure customer satisfaction, the Army must do more to obtain feedback on customer perceived value, however, training must first educate the customer on the reciprocal relationship of each customer's perceived value (i.e., 360 feedback) only then can business results make sense. In other words, a culture must be developed where the senior leaders optimize the system as a whole. A challenge currently is to obtain customers perceived value after they have been trained and guided with the principles for organization transformation. Otherwise, best efforts will not be sufficient to obtain the quantum leap necessary to obtain the AAN end state.

A strong need for quantitative and qualitative measures is required to compete in this economic age.

Aggregate measures such as return on investment (ROI), asset utilization, operating margins, profitability, liquidity, debt to equity ratio, value added per employee, and financial activity measure are appropriate for responding to market performance, business growth and new markets entered.[27]

Human resource results are equally significant if not more important in determining business results.

In the area of financial and market results much can be achieved despite the fact that the Army does not have a profit motive. However, in order to effect change in a new economic era, business (i.e., financial) and market results must apply in order to transform the organization and assists the proper mix of leap ahead and evolutionary capabilities. Army leaders, military and civilian, must better state their case in the media and in the Congress particularly due to the fact that members of these groups least well understand the Army. This is true for the following reasons:

- Lack of military service
- The Cold War threat has been eliminated
- Perceived need for cuts in defense spending
- Changing societal values
- Perceptions of irrelevance of the Army
- Perceptions of no near term competitor.

The reasons stated support the perceived need of some U.S. Representatives to support non-defense related programs. Media relations are important due to the Army's need to state its case regarding actual shortfalls such as end strength (personnel manning). Overall, it is important to get funding for current and new missions.

The CSA states that soldiers are our credentials. This statement highlights the Army's concern for people. Transition comes back to people.

In the final analysis, everything comes back to people. People are not in the organization, they are the organization. The bricks and mortar, machines and computers are there only to leverage the power of those people. Be they soldiers on some outpost far from home, high school teachers, sales associates in a department store, flight attendants, software engineers, machine operators, whatever. It is the people in your organization that make the difference.[28]

In determining human resource results, human systems leadership (HSL) must become a new science that brings together indicators such as climate, surveys, resolutions, Uniform Code of Military Justice (UCMJ) actions, equal opportunity and equal employment opportunity (EO/EEO) complaints, and family support group issues. The indicators must be well being, training and development, work system performance and effectiveness. Again, much of this is viewed as a "touchy feely" human skill which is often the most difficult skill set to master due to the highly complex, highly diverse nature of humans, and the lack of predictability of the human resource asset. This type of asset management is one of our most difficult challenges. It is vital in the transformation.

Remove barriers that rob people of pride of workmanship. These barriers must be removed from two groups of people. One group is management or people on salary. The barrier is the annual rating of performance, or merit rating. . . . The other group is hourly workers, which proceed into herewith. The production work in America is under handicaps that are taking a terrific toll in quality, productivity and competitive position. Barriers and handicaps rob the hourly worker of his birthright, the right to be proud of his work, the right to do a good job. These barriers exist in almost every plant, factory, company, department store, government office in the United States today.[29]

The challenge in this area is to reinvent work system design and process to enable human resource leverage of the tools and technologies required to achieve AAN's objective.

AAN's objective is to provide the Army leadership the raw material for a vision of war, and thus land power's role, in the 30-year future. To accomplish that objective, the AAN process must be continuous, year after year, so that the Army's vision is always extended and linked to developments in other services. Provided it remains solidly connected to technological and organizational development, such a process is the Army's best assurance of a smooth and effective glide path to the future.[30]

This quote highlights the continuous improvement requirements inherit in the AAN process. It is important to apply quality principles to achieve the end state.

Finally, the organization's work system design must integrate supplier-partner performance results. These results must be tied to Army 2010 and AAN. These organizational results allow the organization an opportunity to show internal product or service quality improvements, operational results such as cycle time, productivity, efficiency, and process results not already covered.[31]

LEADING INNOVATION
AND CHANGE

One of the most significant books, *The Fifth Discipline, the Arts and Practice of the Learning Organization.*

that has influenced thinking in the private sector is the work by Peter Senge of the Massachusetts Institute of Technology.

In the long run, the only sustainable source of competitive advantage is your organizations ability to learn faster than its competition.[32]

Senge's study of complex systems highlights the following principles:

- To permanently change a system you have to change its structure.

In any given system there are very few "high leverage points" where one can intervene to produce significant, lasting changes in the behavior of the system.

- The more complex the system, the farther away cause and effect usually are from each other in both space and time.
- It doesn't take very many feedback loops before it gets tough to predict the behavior of a system.
- Neither the high-leverage points nor the correct way to move the levers for the desired results tend to be obvious.
- "Worse before better" is often the result of a change of a high-leverage policy in the "right" direction; therefore any policy change that produces better results immediately should almost always be suspect.[33]

An understanding of systems and the high leverage points in systems is key to leading innovation and change. Senge's work addresses the function of learning in the organization as art and practice. Organizational leaders feel or believe that due to their selection as senior leaders that their job was or is to direct the future course of the organization. Senior leaders must lead to some extent from behind. "When the work is done the people all say, we did it ourselves," Lao Zu, Chinese philosopher.

As dynamic as organizations are, we must make distinctions between information technology and human technology systems.

No one can predict where the information age will lead us. No one can reliably predict whether technology will ultimately enhance or impair the human dimension of senior leadership but one thing is sure – technology is here to stay. Either we master technology or technology will master us.[34]

The organizational learning that Senge speaks about addresses "idea power," the seeds of creativity. Senior leaders do not own creativity. Yes, many are highly creative, however, the greater challenge of senior leadership is to foster the environment for creativity and innovation, then leverage creative power to manage and lead change.

Organizational change is about making alterations to the organization's purpose, culture, structure, and processes in response to seen or anticipated changes in the environment. Strategic management of change is all about identifying and embedding in the organization those changes that will ensure the long-term survival of the organization.[35]

The organizational robustness in the face of pressures in the environment must be led. "Robustness" is:

- The capacity to adopt and maintain competitive advantage
- Openness: the freedom to question one's own beliefs and assumptions
- Resource self-sufficiency: the means needed to put plans into action
- Constituency support: maintaining contact, credibility, and commitment.[36]

As we further address the leadership of innovation and change in the information age or new age, the age of participation is also dawning.

Despite the entry of the idea of participation into main stream business thought, the practice of authentic participation is alive only in small segments of business, education, health care, and government.[37]

Many organizations have adopted employee empowerment programs, but have not fully integrated the programs into the organization's business.

In a participative organization, the entire company's first order of business must be to support frontline workers as individual contributors and as teams. The goal is to ensure that there are no barriers between the people who make and distribute the product and who serve customers, and being the best.38

This former quote highlights the need for participation in the 21st Century organization. The goal again is continuous improvement, productivity, and enhanced market share and/or service delivery.

The latter quote highlights the fact that participation is key in developing a high performance organization. A high performance organization is one where the outputs (i.e., products, services) are greater than the inputs (i.e., raw materials, human resources). Participation helps leverage the inputs and provides ownership (psychic and literal) and commitment to innovation and work processes. Participation is the system for meeting the work place challenges of today and tomorrow.

To achieve the quality, productivity, and innovation needed to compete in today's marketplace, organizations of all types are instituting participative programs from empowerment and self managing teams to total quality management. McLagan and Nel 1998 show that in order for these programs to be effective, they must be part of an overall shift to participative governance involving fundamental changes in values, competencies, management, relationships, leadership, pay systems, structures, controls and information.[39]

In addition, the leader must be cognizant of the multicultural workplace in order to lead innovation and change toward the desired future state. Due to the changing nature of the American workplace, new challenges for leaders exist. Cultural and sub-cultural values influence individuals differently at work. The leader must correct common misinterpretations of cultural behavior in order to build cohesive work teams. The leader must also help employees/soldiers discover how multicultural diversity strengthens the workplace and the organization.

It is also important to note that education and training must be utilized to assist workers in understanding intra group distinctions that focus on world view, values, work style, identity, thinking style, and communication style.[40]

The various intra-group distinctions mentioned often differ in the workplace that has representation of Native Americans, Hispanic Americans, African Americans, Asian Americans, and mainstream Americans.

With workforce diversity, you have a mixture of people who can vary along an infinite number of lines, age, tenure, life style, sexual orientation, education, experience, geographic origin, race, gender – just to name a few possibilities. . . . Leaders must ask themselves several questions that have the potential to optimize the organization as a while. First: Do we have an appropriate mission? Do we have a vision? Do we have sufficient strategic thinking and planning capabilities? Do we have a culture that is congruent with our external, environment, mission, vision, and strategy? . . . The leadership task is to ensure that cultural modifications are made as needed to maintain congruence with the environment and with changes in mission, vision, and strategy.[41]

To lead change, not only should participation be encouraged, but the ability to lead change in a participative, multicultural workplace should be encouraged. Obviously, the leaders' skill, knowledge and abilities must be extraordinary.

The leadership objective is to have a vision, strategy, and culture that are individually congruent with each other, and collectively, congruent with the external environment. Once this congruence is achieved, and if the environment remains stable, leadership relative to managing becomes unimportant.[42]

The leader's responsibility now becomes that of the change agent, or specifically, organization culture change agent. Organizational change and transformation require a science of leadership for a new age.

As they go about their work of facilitating, coordinating, and problem solving, leaders are embedding the sources of meaning into the fabric of the organization. So leading is not an aloof, distant activity, but rather one that covers day-to-day issues.[43]

In the final year of this century, it is apparent that new challenges will await the leadership of the U.S. Army. The senior leaders must have the ability to look ahead, and vision a future state that will continually evolve. Currently, governments are beginning to think more and more like business.[44]

The emergence of culture and values as sources of competitive edge for industrialized nations signals a profound shift in world order.[45]

The world of the future, as seen by many futurists, is less technologically successful but the key predictor of economic success will be the notions of creativity and social responsibility. The future requires us to ask the question: will technology master us or will we master technology? Many of the AAN areas of interests are heavily weighted on the side of technology and not on the human side of the organization. I maintain that it is time for a strategic pause to seek balance.

One might argue that the Army Performance Improvement Criteria (APIC) do not work with combat units, in that combat units are more directed towards tactics and effects rather than efficiencies. However, economics of scale and efficiencies can be related to "effects" in that, damage assessments can obviously be measured. This measurement determines the efficiency of the operation(s). Quality processes enhance the productive capability of the group, team, or unit.

The APIC criteria provides accountability metrics to assess the change. Strategies that can measure the leadership of change based on the overarching strategy. AAN focuses primarily on the technology and the equipment needed to modernize and realize the Army imperatives. Although the human dimension of leading change is neglected, Dr. Douglas Johnson of the Army War College, Strategic Studies Institute has remarked, "it is not sexy." He further maintains that more interest is given to equipment and not the human dimension. The human dimension impacts the human resource challenges, dilemmas in a changing environment which addresses basic qualification requirements, recruitment, training doctrine, leader development and organization effectiveness. Many years ago the Army closed its organizational effectiveness (OE) school. Perhaps more emphasis and direction can enhance APIC and overall OE efforts that institutionalize change and monitor continuous improvement. In addition, it may be prudent to establish, if not already, an organization that leads the change effort and uses APIC criteria to measure change and enhance and chart innovation.

The human dimension must also address combat stressors and the management of conflict. These variables must be addressed at the individual, group, and organization levels. One of the best methods of ensuring the leader development address a violate, uncertain, complex and ambiguous (VUCA) environment, is to begin training and developing personnel in the effects of stress (conflict). For example:

Vigilance deterioration, determinations and inaccurate calculations, faulty reports, slow decisions, inaccurate decisions, misunderstood orders, and misused weapons.[46]

In addition,

Soldiers, leaders and staffs will face problems of reduced efficiency and effectiveness when fighting over extended periods. These conditions will tend to neutralize the potential gains of new war-fighting technologies and force new approaches to the preparation and employment of soldiers, leaders and staff.[47]

The previously mentioned aspects of combat stress (conflict) requires that rigorous training address readiness responsibilities of unit cohesion development.

This development should focus on trust and establishing effective communication throughout the unit.[48]

The following responsibilities relate to senior (organizational) leaders:

The chain of command must ensure that the standard for military leadership are met. Senior leaders must provide the necessary information and resources to the junior leaders to control combat stress and to make stress work for the U.S. Army and against the enemy.[49]

The junior (direct) leader's responsibilities are:

. . . Applying the principles of stress control day-to-day, hour by hour, minute by minute. These responsibilities overlap senior leaders' responsibilities but include parts that are fundamentally 'sergeants business' supported by officers. . . . Each soldier must exercise self-leadership and control stress for self and others.[50]

SERVANT LEADERSHIP

Servant leadership is a concept that will continue to increase in relevance.

The servant leadership concept is a principle, a natural law, and getting our social value systems and personal habits aligned with this enabling principle is one of the great challenges of our lives.[51] . . . Servant leadership emphasizes increased service to others, a holistic ecological approach to work, promoting a sense of community, of togetherness, of connection. That is what the whole future is going to be. It's interdependency, it's connection, and it's the sharing of power in decision making.[52]

To be in service to others is an important concept in enabling others to commit to a vision. In addition, the concept of service to others challenges our historic characteristics of leadership. I believe servant leadership characteristics can also be adapted to the military. In fact, many service leadership characteristics are similar to the leadership characteristics previously mentioned. The following characteristics are essential to the development of servant leaders:

Listening, Empathy, Healing, Awareness, Persuasion, Conceptualization, Foresight, Stewardship, and Commitment to the growth of people, Building community.[53]

The servant leader concept is significant in leading change and innovation. Servant leadership characteristics of listening help the leaders identify and clarify the will of the organization, groups or individual. The ability to empathize (i.e., seek to understand rather than be understood) is critical in leading change. Empathy is most concerned with listening. Healing is a powerful human capability. It flows from empathy and requires that the leader respond to what he or she receives (hears) from the organization, group, and individual. Healing seeks to "repair" harm. Awareness requires that we constantly monitor the "situation" or the environment as climate. "Situational awareness" is key in also monitoring the day-to-day, hour to hour, minute by minute. Leaders at all levels must direct this activity. Persuasion is going to be ever important in the new millennium. Persuasion is a part of a new "skill set" which is replacing coercive authority in the information age. Persuasion is a skill closely related to negotiation, mediation and conciliation. These skills are "key" in consensus building with organizations (i.e., Army commands, interagency) and groups. Conceptualization is a key balance in visioning a future state while keeping a "minds eye" on the day-to-day. Foresight is the ability to "look ahead," the skill of trying to define a likely outcome. Little has been researched on foresight, however, it is key in attempting to predict second and third order effects. Stewardship is holding something in trust for another.[54]

Stewardship requires choosing service over self interest. It further requires openness and persuasion rather than control. Commitment to the growth of people requires that the leader "teach" the led. Commitment to people requires that the leader teach the led the previously discussed leadership principles and encourage participation in the organization, group, individual. Last, but not least, the leaders job is to build community. To break down barriers that divide people based on gender, race, ethnicity, age, and ability. Other barriers that divide people in organizations must be eliminated. The ability to build community is the skill in leveraging difference, leveraging difference is essential in developing high performing organizations. High performance means that outputs are greater than inputs. Servant leadership's time has come now that we are on the threshold of the new millennium. It is essential in leading change an innovation.

CONCLUSION

Making the Army more innovative and responsive requires a variety of leadership and power issues be leveraged. This is highly important in a VUCA environment. The 1998 Army Performance Improvement criteria serves as a planning, assessing, and training tool and further charts expectations for a desired end state. It also highlights best business practices for use in operational and strategic organizational elements.

In addressing AAN, the leverage and influence issues that relate to performance and team development, organization management of process, values, and organization development require that the leader be competent and capable in the following area:

LEADER COMPETENCIES
- Leadership change
- Fostering entrepreneurism
- Gaining resources
- Avoiding destructive relationships
- Building diverse teams
- Avoiding power struggles
- Fostering organization excellence, creativity and innovation

---

Figure 9 Leader Competencies

The challenges faced by strategic leaders in implementing complex and long-range consequential decisions demand that they be sophisticated with respect to issues of leadership, power and influence. The changes that are shaping the nature of work in today's complex organizations require that we develop the political will, expertise and personal skills to become more <u>flexible</u>, innovative and adaptive. Without political awareness and skill we face the inevitable prospect of becoming immersed in bureaucratic infighting, parochial politics and destructive power struggles, which generally retard organizational initiative, innovation, morale and performance.[55]

The value added to the Army will be based on mission accomplishment and business results which lead change to 2025. The organizations mentioned can merge the disciplines of strategic leadership, information management, organizational learning, and effectiveness.

ENDNOTES

1   Dennis J. Reimer, "Leadership for the 21st Century: Empowerment, Environment, and the Golden Rule," Military Review vol. 76, no. 1, (January-February 1996):5.

2   William T. Johnson et al., The Principles of War in the 21st Century: Strategic Considerations (Carlisle, PA: Strategic Studies Institute, August 1995), 1.

3   Department of the Army, Army Performance Improvement Criteria, 1998. Total Army Quality, Leading Change (Washington D.C.: U.S. Department of the Army, 1998), 2.

4   MG Richard A. Chilcoat, Strategic Art: The New Discipline for 21st Century Leaders (Carlisle Barracks, PA: Strategic Studies Institute, 10 October 1995), 1.

5   Ibid., 4.

6   National Defense University, Strategic Leadership, and Decision Making: Preparing Senior Executives for the 21st Century (Washington, D.C.: National Defense University Press, 1997), 8.

7   Ibid., 9.

8   Ibid., 10.

9   Department of the Army, Army After Next FY 99 Campaign Plan (Washington, D.C.: U.S. Department of the Army, 30 Sep 98), 9.

10 Ibid., 4.

11 Ibid., 5.

12 Department of the Army, Army Performance Improvement Criteria, 1998, 1.

13 Vincent Omachonu and Joel E. Ross, Principles of Total Quality (Delray Beach, FL: St Lucie Press: 1994), 117.

[14] Ibid., 124.

[15] Reimer, 6,7.

[16] Department of the Army, Army Performance Improvement Criteria, 1998, 28.

[17] Chairman of the Joint Chiefs of Staff, Joint Doctrine for Information Operations, Joint Publication 3-13 (Washington, D.C.: GPO, 2 July 1997) : 1-25.

[18] Sam Cox et al., "Information Assurance, The Achilles Heel of Joint Vision 2010," Joint Staff Information Assurance Digest. Edition 80, (Armed Forces Staff College, Joint and Combined Officer School, Intermediate Course 98-3, August 10, 1998) : 1-10

[19] Department of the Army, Army Performance Improvement Criteria, (1998), 33.

[20] National Defense University, Strategic Leadership, and Decision Making: Preparing Senior Executives for the 21st Century, 180.

[21] Ibid., 181.

[22] Department of the Army, Army Performance Improvement Criteria, (1998), 37.

[23] Ibid., 105, 106, 107.

[24] Peter Drucker, "The Emerging Theory of Manufacturing," Harvard Business Review, vol. 68 no. 03, (May/June 1990) : 95.

[25] Edwards W. Deming, Out of the Crisis (Cambridge: Massachusetts Institute of Technology Center for Advanced Engineering Study, 1982), 87.

[26] Ibid., 28.

[27] Department of the Army, Army Performance Improvement Criteria, 1998, 49.

[28] Gordon R. Sullivan and Michael V. Harper, HOPE is not a Method – What Business Leaders Can Learn From America's Army (New York: Broadway Books, 1996), 240.

[29] Deming, 77.

[30] Department of the Army, The Annual Report on the Army After Next Project to the Chief of Staff of the Army (Washington, D.C.: U.S. Department of the Army, July 1977) : 8.

[31] Department of the Army, Army Performance Improvement Criteria, 1998, 53.

[32] Tom Gzerwinski, <u>Coping with the Bounds, Speculations on Non-linearity in Military Affairs</u> (Washington, D.C.: National Defense University Press, 1998), 111.

[33] Ibid., 117.

[34] National Defense University, <u>Preparing Senior Executives for the 21st Century</u>, 49.

[35] Ibid., 352.

[36] Ibid., 354.

[37] Patricia McLagan and Nel, Christo, "The Age of Participation," <u>New Governance for the Workplace and the World</u> (San Francisco: Berrett-Koehler Publishers, 1997), ix.

[38] Ibid., 202.

[39] Ibid., 324.

[40] Jaime Wurzel and Pai Young, <u>The Multicultural Workplace, Participant's Workbook, MTI Film and Video</u> (Northbrook, IL: Boston University Press, 1990).

[41] Roosevelt R. Thomas, <u>Redefining Diversity</u> (New York: Amacon, American Management Association, 1996), p. 70.

[42] Ibid., 70-71.

[43] Ibid., 72.

[44] Hamish McRae, <u>The World in 2020, Poverty, Culture and Prosperity</u> (Cambridge: Harvard Business School Press, 1994), 185.

[45] Ibid., 303.

[46] Department of the Army, <u>Leaders Manual for Combat Stress Control</u>, Field Manual 22-55, (Washington, D.C.: U.S. Department of the Army, 1994), 1-6.

[47] Ibid., 1-9.

[48] Ibid., 1-9.

[49] Ibid., 1-9.

[50] Ibid., 1-11.

[51] Lang Spears, ed., <u>Insights on Leadership, Service, Stewardship, Spirit, and Steward Leadership</u>, (New York: John Wiley and Sons, 1998), xiv.

[52] Ibid., xiv.

[53] Ibid., 45.

54 Peter Block, <u>Stewardship</u>, (San Francisco: Berrett-Koehler, 1993), [Pages?].

55 John P. Kotter, "Leading Change: Why Transformation Efforts Fail." <u>Harvard Business Review</u>, vol. 73, no.2, (March-April 1995) : 59-67.

BIBLIOGRAPHY

Block, Peter. Stewardship. San Francisco: Berrett-Koehler, 1993.

Chilcoat, Richard A. Strategic Art: The New Discipline for the 21st Century. Carlisle Barracks, PA: Strategic Studies Institute, 10 October 1995.

Conen, William S. Annual Report to the President and Congress. Washington D.C.: GPO, 1998.

Cox, Sam, Ron Stineare, Tim Dean, Brad Asheley. "Information Assurance, The Achilles Heel of Joint Vision 2010." Joint StaffInformation Assurance Digest. Armed Forces Staff College, Joint and Combined Officer School, Intermediate Course 98-3, August 10, 1998, 1-10.

Deming, Edwards W. Out of the Crisis. Cambridge: Massachusetts Institute of Technology Center for Advanced Engineering Study, 1986.

Drucker, Peter, ed. "The Emerging Theory of Manufacturing." Harvard Business Review. Vol. 68, no. 03 (May/June 1990): [pages?]

The Futurist. "Forecasts, Trends, and ideas About the Future." The Futurist Magazine. Vol. 32, no. 06 {Aug-Sep 1998}.

Gzerwinski, Tom. Coping with the Bounds: Speculations on Non-linearity in Military Affairs. Washington, D.C.: National Defense University Press, 1998.

Harog, Richard J. Government in America. Boston: Houghton Mifflin Company, 1994.

Hoyle, John R. Leadership and Futuring, Making Visions Happen, Thousand Oaks, CA: Corwin Press Inc, 1995.

Johnson, William T. and Douglas V. Johnson. <u>The Principles of War in the 21st Century: Strategic Considerations</u>. Carlisle Barracks, PA: Strategic Studies Institute, August 1945.

Kotter, John P. "Leading Change: Why Transformation Efforts Fail," <u>Harvard Business Review</u>, Vol. 73, no. 2 March/April 1995.

McLagan, Patricia and Christo Nel. "The Age of Participation," <u>New Governance for the Workplace and the World</u>. San Francisco: Berrett-Koehler Publishers, 1997.

McRae, Hamish. <u>The World in 2020, Poverty, Culture and Prosperity</u>. Cambridge: Harvard Business School Press, 1994.

National Defense University. <u>Strategic Leadership and Decision Making: Preparing Senior Executives for the 21st Century</u>. Washington, D.C.: National Defense University Press, 1997.

Omachonu, Vincent and Joel E. Ross. <u>Principles of Total Quality</u>. Delray Beach, FL: St. Lucie Press, 1994.

Petersen, John L. The Road to 2015: Profiles of the Future. Corte Madera, CA: Waite Group Press, 1994

Reimer, Dennis Jr. "Leadership for the 21st Century: Empowerment, Environment and the Golden Rule." Military Review. Vol. 76, No. 01, (January-February 1996) : 5-9.

The Reserve Officer's Association. The Officer: ROA National Security Report, Washington, D.C.: Reserve Officer Association, 1998.

Scales, Robert H. Jr. "Trust, Not Technology, Sustains Coalitions." <u>Parameters: U.S. Army War College Quarterly</u>. Vol. 28, No. 4. (Winter 1998-1999) : 4-10.

Spears, Lang, Ed., <u>Insights on Leadership, Service, Stewardship, Spirit, and Steward Leadership</u>. New York: John Wiley and Sons, 1998.

Stauss, William and Neil Howe. <u>The Fourth Turning: What the Cycles of History Tell Us About America's Next Rendezvous with Destiny</u>. New York: Broadway Books, 1997.

Sullivan, Gordon R. and Michael V. Harper. <u>HOPE is not a Method – What Business Leaders Can Learn From America's Army</u>. New York: Broadway Books, 1996.

Sun Tzu. <u>The Art of War</u>. Translated by Samuel B. Griffin. London: Oxford University Press, 1963.

Swindall, Charles R. The Living Insight Study Bible. Grand Rapids, MI: Zondervan Publishing House, 1996.

Thomas, Roosevelt R. Redefining Diversity. New York: Amacon, American Management Association, 1996.

Toffler, Alvin and Heidi, T. War and Anti-War: Survival at the Dawn of the 21st Century. Boston: Little, Brown, & Company, 1993.

Ueshiba, Morihein. The Art of Peace. Translated by John Stevens. Boston & London: Shambala, 1992.

U.S. Army Strategic Studies Institute. Conference Report: The Role of the Armed Forces in the Americas: Civil Military Relations for the 21st Century. Carlisle Barracks, PA: Strategic Studies Institute, 1993.

U.S. Department of the Army. Army After Next FY 88 Campaign Plan. Washington, D.C.: U.S. Department of the Army, 199

U.S Department of the Army. Army Performance Improvement Criteria: 1998. Total Army Quality, Leading Change. Washington, D.C.: U.S. Department of the Army, 1998.

U.S. Department of the Army. Leaders Manual for Combat Stress Controls. Field Manual 22-55. Washington, D.C.: U.S. Department of the Army, 1994.

U.S. Department of the Army. Military Leadership. Field Manual 22-100. Washington, D.C.: U.S. Department of the Army, 1983.

U.S. Joint Chiefs of Staff. Joint Doctrine for Information Operation. Joint Publication 3-13. Washington, D.C.: GPO, 2 July 1997.

U.S. Marine Corps. Strategy. MCDP 1-1, PCN 142 000007 00. Washington, D.C.: GPO, 1997.

U.S. Military Academy. Edited by The Associates, Officer of Military Leadership. A Study of Organizational Leadership. Harrisburg, PA: Stackpole Books: 1976.

U.S. Special Operations Command. 10th Anniversary History. Headquarters, U.S. Special Operations Command, History and Research Office, MacDill AFB, FL, April 1997.

Van Creveid, Martin. The Training of Officers from Military Professionalism to Irrelevance. New York: The Fresh Press, 1990.

WIRED Magazine. Vol. 6, no. 9, September 1998.

Wilkes, Gene C. <u>Jesus on Leadership</u>. Wheaton, IL: Tyndale House Publishers, Inc., 1998.

Wurzel, Jaime. <u>The Multicultural Workplace, Participant's Workbook,</u> MTI Film and Video. Northbrook, IL: Boston University Press, 1994

Yergin, Daniel and Joseph Stanislaw. <u>The Commanding Heights: The Battle Between Government and the Market Place That is Remaking the Modern World.</u> New York: Simon & Schaster, 1998.

Zhuge, Liang and Liu Ji. <u>Mastering the Art of War</u>. Translated and edited by Thomas Cleary. Boston & London: Shambala, 1995.

CPSIA information can be obtained at www.ICGtesting.com
Printed in the USA
LVOW11s1504190214

374386LV00001B/340/P